KUNG FU

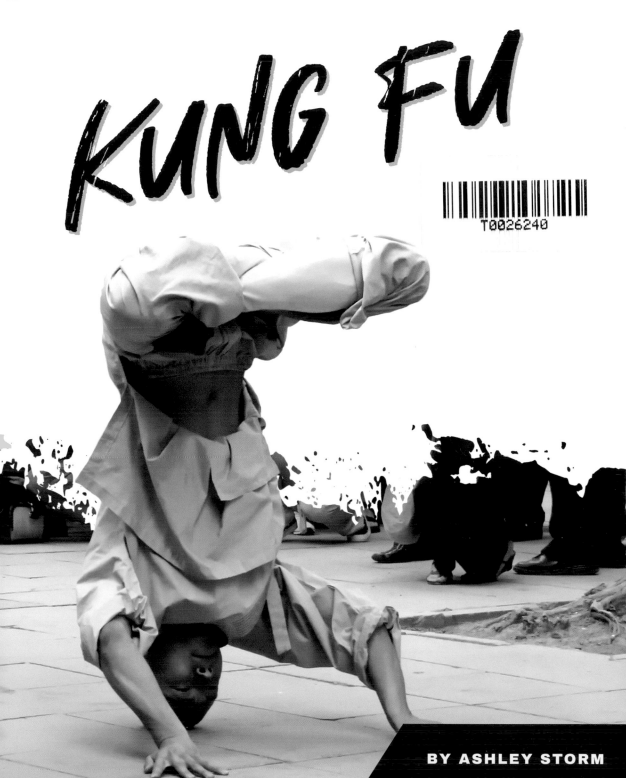

T0026240

BY ASHLEY STORM

Apex is distributed by North Star Editions:
sales@northstareditions.com | 888-417-0195

Produced for Apex by Red Line Editorial.

Photographs ©: Achmad Ibrahim/AP Images, cover; Shutterstock Images, 1, 4–5, 6–7, 8, 9, 10–11, 12, 13, 16–17, 18, 19, 20–21, 22–23, 24–25, 26, 27, 29; Archivio GBB/Alamy, 14

Library of Congress Control Number: 2023910143

ISBN
978-1-63738-766-5 (hardcover)
978-1-63738-809-9 (paperback)
978-1-63738-891-4 (ebook pdf)
978-1-63738-852-5 (hosted ebook)

Printed in the United States of America
Mankato, MN
012024

NOTE TO PARENTS AND EDUCATORS

Apex books are designed to build literacy skills in striving readers. Exciting, high-interest content attracts and holds readers' attention. The text is carefully █████ed to allow students to achieve success quick██ ████ditional features, such as bolded glossary words for difficult terms, help build comprehension.

TABLE OF CONTENTS

CHAPTER 1

WARRIOR MONKS

It's early morning at the Shaolin Temple in China. The **monks** are already awake. They are practicing kung fu.

The Shaolin Temple is located in north-central China. It was founded in 495 CE.

The Shaolin monks practice doing sets of moves together.

The monks stand in rows. They punch, spin, and kick. Their movements are fast and strong. They are graceful, too. It almost looks like they're dancing.

FAST FACT

Some monks begin training at age three.

The monks practice three times throughout the day. In between, they take breaks to eat, study, and do chores. They repeat this pattern every day of the week.

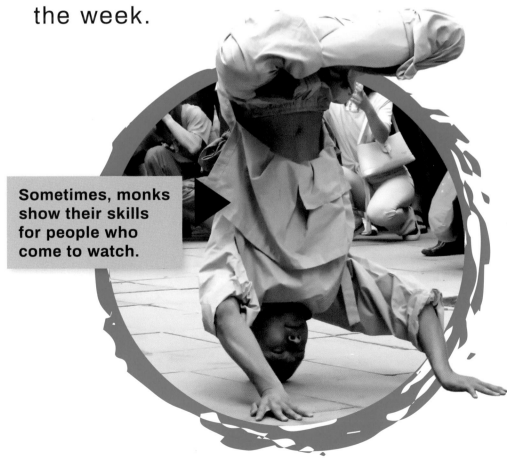

Sometimes, monks show their skills for people who come to watch.

The monks' meals often include vegetables, rice, nuts, and beans.

DO NO HARM

The Shaolin monks are Buddhists. Their religion focuses on peace. Buddhists try not to harm others. So, they don't eat animals. Instead, they eat plant-based foods, such as fruit and grains.

CHAPTER 2

KUNG FU HISTORY

Monks have practiced kung fu at the Shaolin Temple for more than 1,500 years. But kung fu is even older. It comes from ancient China.

People in China began practicing kung fu more than 2,000 years ago.

At first, soldiers used kung fu to train for battle. Over time, many kung fu styles developed. Some used weapons. Others focused on building strength and **self-control**.

Kung fu teaches fighters many ways to attack and defend.

Traditional Chinese swords called dao can be used in kung fu.

FAST FACT

Some forms of kung fu use spears, swords, darts, or knives.

These styles spread to Japan and other countries. In the 1900s, people began making kung fu movies. Kung fu gained even more fans.

BRUCE LEE

Bruce Lee was an actor. He lived from 1940 to 1973. He studied and taught kung fu. He also created jeet kune do. This new style blended kung fu, boxing, and fencing.

Kung fu movies grew especially popular in the 1970s and 1980s. Bruce Lee starred in many.

CHAPTER 3

TYPES OF KUNG FU

Today, people do many types of kung fu. Styles are often split into two groups. External styles build strength and speed for fighting. Internal styles focus more on the mind.

People who want to learn kung fu have many options.
There are hundreds of different styles.

In Shaolin kung fu, people learn hundreds of moves. They're grouped into sets called forms.

Shaolin kung fu is the most famous external style. Wing Chun is another. In it, fighters move their fists and feet quickly.

In Wing Chun, fighters do many quick punches in a row.

Tai Chi is the most common internal style. Students move and breathe carefully. They focus on stretching and being flexible. They often **meditate**, too.

In the 2020s, more than 300 million people practiced Tai Chi.

IMITATING ANIMALS

Some kung fu moves and styles are based on animals. They **imitate** how different creatures move and fight. Examples include tigers, cranes, leopards, and snakes.

CHAPTER 4

KUNG FU TODAY

People of all ages practice kung fu. Some use it for exercise. Others want to learn **self-defense**. Many take classes at **martial arts** schools.

Tai Chi can help people build strength and lower their stress.

Some people go to **competitions**. They often do a style called wushu. It is a mix of ancient kung fu and modern rules.

FAST FACT

Top athletes go to the World Kung Fu Championships. This event takes place every two years.

Wushu was created in 1949. It is designed for competing, not real fighting.

There are two main types of wushu. In wushu sanda, pairs of people fight. They kick, punch, and throw each other. In wushu taolu, people perform **routines**.

In wushu sanda, fighters score points for kicks and hits. The person with the most points wins.

In wushu taolu, points are based on how hard each move is and how well the person does it.

TAOLU

In wushu taolu events, people kick, leap, and spin. These moves show their power and skill. Some taolu routines include weapons. People hold swords, spears, or staffs.

COMPREHENSION QUESTIONS

Write your answers on a separate piece of paper.

1. Write a sentence that explains the main idea of Chapter 3.

2. Which style of kung fu would you be most interested in learning? Why?

3. Which is an internal style of kung fu?

    A. Shaolin

    B. Wing Chun

    C. Tai Chi

4. How was kung fu first used?

    A. for fighting battles

    B. for competing in events

    C. for performing routines

5. What does **graceful** mean in this book?

*They are **graceful**, too. It almost looks like they're dancing.*

    A. fast and choppy
    B. smooth and flowing
    C. full of long pauses

6. What does **championships** mean in this book?

*Top athletes go to the World Kung Fu **Championships**. This event takes place every two years.*

    A. an event for the very best athletes
    B. an event for very young children
    C. an event that happens each week

Answer key on page 32.

河南省嵩山少林寺武术馆

GLOSSARY

competitions
Events where people try to beat others in a sport.

fencing
The sport of fighting with swords.

imitate
To copy.

martial arts
Skills used for fighting or self-defense.

meditate
To calm or focus the mind.

monks
People who are part of a religious group and follow strict rules about how to live.

routines
Sets of moves done in a certain order.

self-control
The skill of managing your thoughts, feelings, and actions.

self-defense
Ways to fight back or stay safe if attacked.

TO LEARN MORE

BOOKS

Faust, Daniel R. *Kung Fu*. New York: PowerKids Press, 2020.

Krohn, Frazer Andrew. *MMA: Heroic History*. Minneapolis: Abdo Publishing, 2023.

Peterson, Susan Lynn. *Legends of the Martial Arts Masters*. North Clarendon, VT: Tuttle Publishing, 2019.

ONLINE RESOURCES

Visit **www.apexeditions.com** to find links and resources related to this title.

ABOUT THE AUTHOR

Ashley Storm has written more than 30 books for children and teens. She lives in Kentucky with her husband, three mischievous cats, and a flock of bossy backyard chickens who peck on the door to demand treats.

INDEX

ANSWER KEY:
1. Answers will vary; 2. Answers will vary; 3. C; 4. A; 5. B; 6. A